SCHERZOS BENJYOSOS

Scherzos Benjyosos

Keston Sutherland

THE LAST BOOKS   AMSTERDAM/SOFIA

Published in 2020 by The Last Books
Amsterdam, the Netherlands and Sofia, Bulgaria

www.thelastbooks.org

Designed and typeset by Phil Baber
Printed by Tallinn Book Printers

ISBN 978-94-91780-32-5

CONTENTS

Sinking Feeling

No refuge! No appeal!
                        Sink with me then,
We two will sink on the wide waves of ruin,
Even as a vulture and a snake outspent
Drop, twisted in inextricable fight,
Into a shoreless sea.

I

Dear secret object, I made a swing for you at last, lying awake in pieces, a cantilever strewn with fur, implicit as brain fluid, as though once, I had to have been redistributed in a system of tranches, a network of trays, or to have this flotilla of levels, so that the icon that would be dipped in and out of view, as I push you and you fly round in a spiral, could be of girders sensitively decomposed into the relic of a helix, eyes in a cup suspended in the equivalent of space that, if you like, is split into one half becoming nothing and the other half becoming the room we are in, where I was at work at the usual place and there was some kind of event going on like a festival or celebration of some kind and people or what represented people or the bodies of people had come to be there from around the country. The atmosphere was bright with swerves of levity and cheer, people made an effort to dress up. That woman who used to work there on a part time contract several years back, Haifa, was there, wearing water, and she seemed high on the occasion. She said, I have asthma, ich habe asthma, j'ai de l'asthme. I was moved on past an office whose door was wide open and though I did try to look as though I was not looking in but just happening to be resting my teeth on the illegible crest cut into the cantilever filled for that second with exquisite cubic zirconia filed down to spell out the distress signal dear secret object you never give I could not look and then saw Lazarus inside. She had shaved her head. The hair already gone was also infinitely coming away in clumps. Someone from the department was hosting her. I hurried past this open door because I didn't want to speak to her or be tied up in dialogue with whatever represented her through her getting to say to everyone that I was there, though I knew it was likely she would know. I went into a wide. Time was you could say but can I help you with that can I get that for you prodigal in distanced ice to split or wring. I went into a wide open space that was neither inside nor outside, neither a room nor the world beyond a room, but like a flight deck or the top of a high building. From as far as you could hurl your medals the voice boomed back, I need more of this medication, ich brauche mehr von diese Medikamente, j'ai besoin de plus de ces médicaments. In front of this part of me is an expanse of space, a distance whose wish is to be stretched indistinctly toward what may look like a beach or coast of pale gold sand, misty and glittering, though I could not see any water. Juwairiyah, or Juwayriyah, *in cute curanda*, states the truth to the twisted reed, I was bitten, ich wurde gebissen, j'ai été mordu, and now I am drowning. Behind me, now I find a way to turn again to look, was a stack of what previously could represent pallets from a warehouse, or else some kind of school PE equipment, such as the towers of mats that would keep in a school gym and be pulled out to cover up the hard floor during gymnastics classes. Like the people come dressed as irritant floaters impossible to scratch out of your eyes bouncing about the world as briefly hot as squash balls, these mats or pallets too were indistinct, though not in the way calculated to exaggerate your curiosity to know why and what they were there, or who they were. Later I saw. Protonation states torqued into cranial prostheses now deactivating yearning for what makes you deep or true. A man and a woman. Actionable sex veined with obsidian and scaffolds of elastic rotted out in Vukovarsko-Srijemska. Later I saw a young couple, a man and woman in what represented their twenties, walk together hand in hand past the swing I made for you over to behind the towers of warehouse pallets or folding gymnastics mats, in effect advertising their intention of locating a secluded spot in my rear in which to have deliberate sex. To left and right the space concluded in the usual walls, but they are not close to me and I have no feelings about them. I even thought I could not give a fuck if they are there. There was a desk. That you cannot get in since the entrance is the obstacle itself is what it means for life to end at emptiness. Despite the space. Then to move it through a doorway blocked up with evacuated footholds now laid flat for sliding under you get in. There was a desk or table here in what despite the space from which closeness had been torn out but was still streaming away was still there to playact the middle of the room and when I was standing at this desk in silence repeating, the pain started here and goes to here, der Schmerz wandert von hier nach dort, j'ai mal d'ici à là, I felt irritable, under a stupid pressure, weighted down, as even you dear secret object might feel too if you had some pressing work to complete that made you forget yourself but the environment was too incidental to permit it to be completely done, which was true, because the space was not enclosed enough, not close enough, to feel like a real office or other bounded space of production in which a purpose could be identified and the potentialities slumbering in the breast of man activated so that the play of natural forces could be subjected to the sway of his own power, but also because people kept coming in and out and lying around on the floor and sitting at other tables and talking, and one of them was pushing his toe into my asshole, which was frustrating to me because I felt that the space that for what unfathomable reason I do not know was not able to be enclosed and in which therefore my purpose in being in it could not be expressed was nonetheless my space, if not because it was dedicated to me or my purpose or because I positively owned it, then just because I needed it more, or because I had a use for it that was the most urgent, or because I am crying, though I think I also could sense that somewhere inside me what preserved the shape of my private interior in that space without closeness in it where no object is close to any other object I may not have cared and that I was just acting up for you, my object. A drowned body. For whose surface bodies perforate determines what limb will be saved and what with poignancy piled on the rest in peace. Sitting in a low position. It is immaterial so long that only alternately crystalline and deliquescent words cut into it. Another table. As the Tuareg leave you get a practical sensation unrelated to the scorched umbilicus you say is squid. A drowned body was there sitting in a low position at another table, cross-legged on the floor as people who are still alive used to sit when eating at an authentic Japanese restaurant by the harbour in Nagasaki. The body was distraught and wanted to say why this was so but also it was trying to avoid talking about it in the way that the drowned do, as though it could only ever be tiresome and obnoxious to be dragged into a dialogue that might risk disturbing a surface of emotion always only just now at last ironed flat and placated like a baby who is a nightmare to get to sleep, and then not only because there were other people or bodies representing other people that narrowed in the usual way to an anonymous background to our potential but obstructed intimacy, lying around on the floor and fucking about distractingly in the background. One of them was a long, loping man on the floor behind me who kept pressing his foot against my ass and sticking his toe into my asshole and lower back, whether quite by chance or else by accident or fate I could not tell but anyhow over and over again, saying, it hurts here, hier tut es weh, j'ai mal ici, until I turned round and snapped him into a pyramid of goat, heroin, wind and rain, flush with the relief that always comes with consciousness of my status and power and grieved to think that he could be here in this space at all. This drowned. Then the output was not drowned in complex numbers simulating proxies for adjustment to prop up reality. Body intimated. Since evading shipwreck to be mauled with water cannon at the border of Bakondi's Hungary is not for you. Dying of an incurable. Not but that when later stung or touched into the gulf upon your back in any time reserved against its warped WO2 tarpaulin scored o in 12103142 A3 a trachea that is now hyperventilating. This drowned body intimated to me that an ex-partner of his was dying of an incurable disease and that he had just heard that things had got worse for her. I sympathized with him admirably and tried to encourage him to speak only if he would like to, but he had a mouth full of water and seemed obstinately determined to be incapable of saying anything that got past the wisecracks and pleasantries. Then suddenly you were there. You were wearing. Lateral to now exfoliated implants how else be discrepant pumped up to the empty but erotic word. You were wearing a black cotton top and dark jeans. We are very close. In that space we are the only thing that is close. We were. Scratched into the window whose impediment of glass now gripped interior now flexed to cracking too fast to expel. We were standing in an embrace, but at the same time I was different, disembodied, and could look on from a distance, and from that point I could see only you, not myself, despite how I had intended to pay a visit to myself, though I knew that in reality you were not alone, that you too are on a visit to yourself, however far, and that I am there too. The coast representing the distance at the front grew intensely bright and lustrous as we held each other and filled the space with gold and yellow light. It really felt as though the room itself was surging and billowing, or disintegrating and reforming, or like a balloon full of water, but at the same time what was apocalyptic about this seemed to mean us no terror, it did not ask us to fear what it would mean to come to an end or be split apart. We talked about how it was going to be possible for us to be married at last. We wanted to feel valid. We wanted to be simple. We wanted to be so simple that even people who could watch the 2015 GOP debates at the Coors Event Center in Colorado could understand us without slitting each other's jugular veins and carotid arteries with sponges full of caramelized phlegm like the butchers of Deir al-Zour. We seemed to know that this was going to happen and we spoke about it as though it had always been a plan but things from outside the room had prevented it from being fulfilled. In particular. True when not returning to what after all is not the only future more annihilating to be torn out of. In particular we were worried about how to tell each other that we had always known that we would do this, once the time had actually arrived. There was a sense that the realisation of a life that had been expected for us and that we deserved to be able to live was always bound to be difficult and painful, and we didn't know how to get there, or where it was, when our present reality contained so many distracting complications and other people or bodies representing other people, and other feet or bodies representing other feet, and other assholes or bodies representing other assholes, and perhaps other people or the bodies representing them or the thought of those bodies was part of what distance itself could be made to mean here, where bits of distance in the raw could be picked up everywhere, sprinkled on the tongue, twisted between the fingers like a reed, let fall from the fist like bubbles, or made to protrude in a horizontal bar from a vertical stay, and where nothing felt close enough, where nothing could be closed, and yet where nothing was without an end or unbound either, where people could wander about exchanging ideas like, I fell from a from a height, ich bin abgestürzt, je suis tombé d'une certaine hauteur, and now I am drowning, but where the limits in both directions seemed inescapably symbolic, the one an inescapably transparent symbol of a childhood represented in stacked equipment for the safety of the child body during its obligation to be regimented in exercise, equipment that begins and concludes the scheduled recreation of the child body by being taken out and put away in stacks, as well as, at the same time, an inescapably transparent symbol of an adolescence spent wading under and among warehouse pallets that facilitate the storage of what lies in wait ready to be taken out and packaged and sold once somebody wants it, but what until the moment that somebody does actually want it, supposing anyone ever does, must remain a stock of commodities in aspic or paralysis outside the circuits of valorization, beyond even a limit case of the pathetic fallacy such as a cloud in the shape of Farmakonisi or the Syrian bodies washed up near there, and the other, the limit in front, an inescapably transparent symbol of paradise and death at once, the unknown shore rigged up as a garishly explicit fresco of what it cannot hurt to call meaning, and yet breathtaking still and of a gravity that overwhelms the space of existence, throwing out the interior floor and air like dislocated shoulders, for you dear secret object, who are at once its agony and its anaesthesis, unbreathable as meaning and the kiss of life itself. That you cannot get in since the entrance is the obstacle itself is what it means for once to end at emptiness. Then to move it through a doorway blocked up with evacuated footholds now laid flat for sliding under you get in. Then at either side the walls too indistinct to mean anything or be symbolic enough except through being made to keep their distance, which is ours too, or to have any role in what is the meaning of their dissipation except by later being cast as its periphery, drowned out in the surging, irritation, bodies in the way, transparency and representations of transparency, reticence and gravity as though in their reality there were no other movement, or any body left, or only one.

II

This is the kind of thought it pays to have. The thought
I can't fucking do this any more that gets you nowhere is
free. The locution Floor lockout A on B on C on, thought
over by the open border of the teller station in undrying
acrylics nobody is denying is not real, crossing whose
core of rim law gets shot of an obscene heart, it will be
remembered, memory lubricates oblivion, blindness gets
you nowhere, dear scene forever erupting, dear secret
object, as of this hour, let float between the wicker gaps
in sanity, in grainy resolution on the patched-up wall in
knots projected fire, being given some spending money
by the heron is not what you dreamed you would end
up as, but pulling the caravan and its profiled content of
characters across the final form of the map, tacking west
to east, covering the distances too fast, pedagogically, as
though the sort of reconstituted people who alone can
be counted on to watch, paid in thought, should never
be trusted to depend on it that any progress is being
made for people like them unless it is sped up to prove
it, who arrive finally at a restricted edge or line that for
what obscure reason could not be guessed could not be
crossed, though others in front had plunged in and were
going on submerged in that dark nacreous water, getting
ahead of you, while knowing that you are stuck, and while
being berated by a frantic old man decked in inflexible
shreds of glass, who says that he has to go further right
away, that he cannot stay here a moment longer, that he

cannot pretend to be satisfied with where he is, like his mother who had watched *Elf* and thought fuck it that will do, whose stick insects and crickets that I own are in fact me, charmed to be as one the brain containing their appearance broke what contained me and I was lost in what could not be found replaced with an equivalent because it sounds different, whose childhood dog's head is in real time being shaved as a knee-jerk remedy for the inadvertent amputation of her misremembered point, and that half largely barren of material virginities, fanned to anneal its plumes of sunlit ash in the past it is dying to shift, exhaled into asphyxiating human conventions whose just redecorated walls are still drying, that no suspension of the progressive-slide drawer need go hungry, on his account, and that, barring your progress, a broken mind stuck to the cavity eternity still borders on in the preliminary form of pictures of the faces that still vacate it every time the static or revolving back is turned for good to have another person who had loved you go away need not starve, or degenerate into a secret, but that it could be free to live according to its needs repurposed in the fantasy of shadowy desire and paralysis terminable and interminable, in solitary confinement, like Theresa May's life, or so I imagine, he says, I say, mistaking the social consequences of a great political career measurable in thousands of ruined lives for knowledge of the human individual underneath who is *chaque fois unique*. For since the loss forever of the people that you love is not perfectible by relocation yet, the irony is that this is the very void that takes you for granted, thinking, I was born in a market in elastic scalpels stretched to and saturated in ecstasy, adding, I was ravaged with serenity, I do not underestimate infatuation with the infinity that is conceivable even now while reaching out, touching base, and making secret people come, imprecating to that end and praying to you that the caravan be tried on the water and carried just past the edge that you are the one put there to know cannot be crossed, eyes flashing, gesticulating in invaluable desperation, to look on in sporadic horror as the heads almost already too far in front creep forward and fan out involuntarily over the outstretched bulging surface.

III

Not the way you move, but in, where, past desire, that,
before the painless, adjacent extinction, first lasts forever,
someone is there, who, for now, stranded in your touch,
in flight across its furthest stretch, to here, cups its hand to
intimate, bid its ruffling gales subside, too far in to surge
wide of, as, but I am just thinking, headlong into the lake,
storming out, for what, without a head, exhaled at will,
sunk in sexual aqueous film, blows out the interiorities, the
lot, the orange on the fire stairs, the idiopathic, existing to
wish to be picked, persevere, to be shined, when, for the
hundredth time cut loose, once they reappear, everyone,
being almost there, so that, in sound, not less immaterial
than rafts of polystyrene or Rohingya rehydrated into
stateless entities, because of the multitude of spermatic
reasons, right this way, anxious to tear reality the fuck out,
in case its top blisters and is peeled, climaxing, falling off,
being repossessed, up to the elbow, where, laced with
you, quarterly projections, attachable into the notches
rear fins, worried that my heart would explode, a point
is traced, do not go for this you lip-read stitched into the
air you wish to empty but will take for now obstructed as
it is, or lost, because reached, pulling away, wherein that,
beyond nothing, stuck to the wall, speaking your mind,
what it took to find you loves you too it says in this voice
I am not far anywhere now feel for me come here go slow,
tell me the one about this, about you, that, rephrased by
everybody coming at the same time in a knot, echoes in

the entrance core of every human void, that, here too
fast rotating, shattered, fine, unfolded, the extremities
are key, disappearing, the difference makes no difference
at all, the difference makes no reference to this, for you
who grease the Turks to round up the exoplanets from
PSR1257 + 12 B to μ Arae c to fuck up Russia and give
the fascists their hard-on, buy a window for the YPG,
pinch the streams of mutilated and traumatized stagnant
labour into jets, shot into the flooded basement, where
slavery is buoyant, to fill it up, and where even now it is
rammed, like unknown faces, come into my veins, right
through this spike, that, this spareBu, where, I broke we
but, happy torn out this gap in the stop throat's head
put on updated defamiliarization techniques to allow for,
investigating new ways of navigating an increasingly
commodified infosphere, on your knees, that, as anyone
who sees you there, who, seeing as you are, the strap on
your shoulder, any flap of cytoplasm and its once vacated
limit to a life is wasted if this clinches what you bear, what
else are potentials for organic solidarity with driftwood
drilled down through the leaping hull for when not that,
how you turn to look back, how the hands that you use,
that I love, how I know to do, this is real or true and you
are touch, you are height, you are breath, and you are
the light, that I know, that I am keeping at this distance,
how do you stay there, that I am made to bear it, now
you are away, the light fall on your head, how it is there,
how the wish is here or close, you are everything, you
are something, you are nothing, you are most things, you
are just a few things, you are one particular thing, you are
that one particular thing, and you are the beginning, you
are the middle, you are the end, you are just after the start,
you are getting closer to the end, you are not moving
from the start, you are that particular not moving from
the start, far away from what you never left, everything is

still the beginning, though something is the middle, and nothing is the end, inflated into concrete fate or pegged to balusters of air where you are made to stop, look back, go on, I am here looking at you and you are there doing it, seeing how you do, the strap on your shoulder, the eyes you abandon, that I use, how I know to, in a way, or not, for now, for you.

Scherzos Benjyosos

I

I am sitting writing this in a bar, doing what in drug and alcohol addiction support groups is called 'defining a private world', according to their poster next to the church opposite the Mash Tun, where I first met my love, and therefore where, in effect, the origin of this voice is deposited, across from the staircase up to the Therapy Centre, where I am between five and ten minutes early, in order to be sitting thinking when I am called, where a voice that is not mine but is inside me starts saying unkind things, like this time it is the proprietor of the Gathering Zone, who had died where people are shocked and confused, not because she was young, or not yet over life when people have to die, or really do it, no, she was old, and still in that time, we are not there yet, be patient, because when we do die it is a shock and it is confusing, not someone like her who had seemed, obviously not immortal but, without seeing how she did it, inherent in life, somehow, the one there for the taking, and for the not being able to take, take my life, strangle me in your veins, forever going on about how she is done with being told what to do and how to live her life and what to eat for tea and where to be in the afternoon prior to debasement down into the pre-reality saved for early evening, before reality sets in, one night, and is not going to be dictated to on the topic of drift or extracted from starvation real, fake, or mental, having been a menial, but is past being about to eat what she is told or made to stop fixating on spiralling specks of adhesive and teak picked off a cuticle without end voiding the skin across the sky or thumb might sting or bleed a bit, if that is what she wants then she will do it, for a change, shut the fuck up, assembled in a hall, cross-legged, sexual, gasping mud, *satura nos*, to all appearances induced on the brink of disintegration, never before, afterward, once, wide-eyed as we know, saying how, why, when, why her, what now, how much, where to now, where are you, does it work, where the fuck are you, calm out of panic, rewritten by a door, salivating code, say no more, because there is nothing to worry about, shut the fuck up, recite me the symbols, and tracing the bars with suboptimal wicker a likewise unlickable finger of mine, unique as all the pigs in Saxony, I said back to her, people live, do their best, for a while, carry on, in their bit of bind, they are somewhere, sometimes they are nearby, swept away, longer than pain, because gone, others fill in, and as I said this I grew conscious, just as in the memory of a dream, that it was hurtful and frightening, that I was carving a scoop of our common head out, the one we already share, like with an ice cream scoop, one with a button in the handle, and then as if by magic trick a note from you appeared, in my head and in my hands which now live in my head, and it was addressed to me, and it read, Hey little Christian, always fussing about the same others, last night you took care of us all, until you passed out, it was good but next time you need to not do anything, just keep still, let it go, shut the fuck up, and it was the kindest thing I had heard, fluted, unfeatherbeddable, or if not the kindest anyhow the most considerate breath of mind I had felt, wafting with the most uninsistently caressing brush of tongue or hair over a retina caked in ski lifts that I had not needed to blink out or immediately lacerate and die, so thank you, because it made me look sideways and see another man who will be important later get up, though he could lie down too, or slump, and signal, in secret, that he was not about to miss this opportunity to stride down the aisle and officiate over the death of this person whom however he had never met, though he might have heard of her, in his way, a way likely to be painful for everyone, not to say a waste of time, because he would assume that he had the more or less God-given authority to deliver the concluding remarks, originally good for everything, and when they arrived they would be the same for everybody, in substance that here was a person who might well have been good or turned out kind or positively annihilated with love and conscience but that this was immaterial because the only thing that matters is being a poet, and by looking at him as he stood up and was about to do this, sideways, with your eyes flowing through my soul, I could prevent it, by turning to face the front, where the world is, so thank you, and thank you also for being on the other side of the thin partition, last night, when I should have been blown up, lightminded, skipping life, when my rage should have pressed the back of my head against their old room's edge with the indented circles on, but instead I was just irritated and didn't know, because nobody told me, as the loud hateful music was blasted out everywhere, that I couldn't find, and I thought it was you but to my credit I eventually knew it was me, right as I noticed the incredible massive stereo next to my bed behind the partition with those separate layers that you used to want to get, and instantly set about switching them off, one by one, the tape deck, the CD player, the amplifier, but getting nowhere, because it was the radio, because I never got to choose the music, because I have never made it loud enough, because it was never my turn, because who else was even listening but me, because there was no one else there, but for the proprietor of the Gathering Zone, who, allowing for the intrinsic heterogeneity of populations, pleasantly enough, it is a professional manufacturer of all type of slewing bearings and non-standard bearings,

heavy and large slew bearings, special used bearings, and
non-standard bearings, integrating research, relying on
the largest production base, for potential technical ability,
she used to say, whose glance did erst the wounds of love
anoint, and we have advanced technical equipments, and
we have perfect inspection equipments, and we have
strong technical strength, and experienced professional
staff, dead, no surprise there, a spirited team, rotting like
chipboard in Bovril, and I am sorry that I woke you up,
I didn't know how thin it was, I knew you were there
but I know that it is a different time zone there, I didn't
think you would be awake, I thought it would not hurt
to disturb you, I didn't know it was me, I didn't say a
word because I couldn't, because how could I, how could
you, and because it was just music, and because I didn't
pick it, and because it was just for now, and because I did
turn it off, and because I did stop making you eat your
vegetables, and because I did stop kicking you in the back
and telling you that you are dying, in effect, all the time,
obsequies to the gale, but am incapable of opening my
mouth without a gulf stream of spicules of amethyst and
safety pins tied down in ribbon flurrying out to spite you,

    I lay down in your arms obscurely stuck and horizontal
    On my eyes as if torn out to cancel visibility,
    Only the hinge of that body glowed where love's least reparable

    Shadow content looped your hand, dear far away you.
    It's so rare to be touched with any meaning that the instant
    Doesn't do away with soon as memory is ready,

    Pointing at the buildings on the fire escape in May,
    Conscious of the legs your mother had you to stick out on.
    Because her promises are in reality unbreakable,

Everything you want will come back as the inability
To love it for the way it can't be held, or hold you
Close to life too distant for the fucked head to go on with.

I put the symbol to my lips and try to be a tunnel.
The tip goes in easy but there's a word stuck under it
Impenetrable to the burnt out mouth it still cracks open,

I thought of you all day in other words and went to bed
Wanting you to do it for me again. My body is lonely,
Lost, trying to get out, stripped to applicability.

During the past so many years, Fill not my life with
torture to the end, there once was a corner, part of the
job, polymorphously ordinary, for all the world as if that
had been going on now for a while, by that point, that
has to become a name, that you once hid there, to exist
without you, as if you had gone away, and told it to wait
for you to come back, and never to let you forget that it
is waiting. Each time you speak you ask for the name,
the better to be moved on. But it is slurred, unheeded,
left out by the earful. The name is lost. Not really, the
name is a word: clearinghouse. The name is scenario, /,
notional 0.944. Or Ben. That will do, that's fine for now,
even to have been going on with, as if possibly, once
you're done jimmying yourself, repeating, you're scared
of the foreseeable, you're going blind with love. As an
example, imagine that 'A' buys protection on Amgen. It
is as if we who are or whoever is almost not there are
or is almost meant not to be there. And it is as if being
almost meant not to be there, behind the square, that
is now on the floor, or anyhow, at floor level, possibly
hovering, sheer and rhomboid, means for the first time
now that we don't have to find a way out. Or Ben. And

it is as if not having a way out or Ben is fascinating, as its meaning is screened for time, and all the time the first time shows up. But also as if fascination is in danger. It is as if it may not be safe for fascination, as if the object or source of fascination could not, probably, be what it thinks it is, or not only what it thinks it is. As if not having a way out were not really there, anyhow, any more than the way out itself is, but as if something else, something worse, were there. As if something a lot worse had to be there, surely, if, as you think, fascination is, now, only a way of hiding as if running away. As if being very fascinated with not having a way out were nothing but what secret Ben screws up like crepe paper to thicken or knit up in hundreds of angles that it would be wrong to sit down and calculate except in a horrific psychosis, dotted with boring bees. Cyclosis spikes, speak for yourself, let yourself go, boss of cock-blocked God, Ben-ho. And it is as if this specific act of violence, itself already the violent screwing up of what is too easily screwed up by violence like crepe paper into a molested cavern of glittering obliquities, were like pushing someone out the window. At last. For it comes as a great relief to be able to do that, at last. As if there it is and all you do is push. Think of a person. As for such catalepsies of the individual as that person, there are only so many times you can go up to them and smear shit in their face and say oh shit sorry I got shit in your face, it was me, or ask permission to recite to them a complete list of towns beginning with the letter C, before you have to tear their world apart, pat dry the remainder, and kick them in the face straight in the stylomandibular ligament, because the fight is on its way, millions, and it's not enough for our point to be better than theirs, that's so fucking easy, we have to be better at fighting too, so that we can win, and we have to know what violence really is, better than they do, and like

it more, and find a way to love it, for the sheer pleasure
of doing what is atrocious but necessary, and we have to
grind their soul of pure *can't* in a mincer, as that person
the catalepsy's eyes bodaciously cream out the nozzle
like bloodshot ringworm of blossoming Play-Doh, to
form a tassel, or sprig, of shit, a hundred buds, that with
a heavy heart we will cause to be snipped off, with a set of
nail-clippers that we were given for Christmas once, and
tossed out the window, that you see for yourself is open,
to where it will come to rest on an obelisk, or moon, of
shit, optionally prone in light, and where it will sprout up
into a billion festoons of the sorry rhododendrons of shit.
But it is as if before you can push anyone out you have to
be sprung up or ejected out of the chair and on to your feet
and clean through a visionless, jellied wall or meniscus
that you know will not ever be able to be reversed back
through because once anything is on the other side of it
it will have ceased to exist. And it is as if its once having
ceased to exist will mean that you have ceased to exist
too, not once, but twice, three times, a hundred times, a
thousand times, or an infinite number of times. Or not
a number of times at all. But it would be wrong not to
try, or it is as if it would. And it is there, that is, really,
here, where we are, all of us, you, Ben, me, that person,
clearinghouse, the sky, apparently behind, but almost as
if not meant to be, as if almost none of us were there,
here to see the square, huddled, or inculcate its outline, at
all, blue-edged, stipulatory, dictatively slanting, we even
look like it, that it is not safe, and that fascination, but that
is obviously the wrong word, is veneficious, the keener
the worse, when there is not or cannot be a way out left
to have, or be cared about, except by being scoured until
it is annihilated, and that this open and shut, veneficious
fascination that is nothing but what is contriturated in
the fist, splitting with bees, like crepe paper randomly

imploded, into a grotto of misspent reflexes and psychotic lustrifications, that could only be the cover for something worse, and that is nothing else but a way of hiding as if running way, saying, you can't see me so I can't see you, out loud, were that possible, that is really like pushing somebody out of a window, even while, as you stare straight at it without blinking, the window slips off the wall and gracefully undulates up to the ceiling, then over to the other wall, then over to the other wall, then down the sofa, then, in no time, on to the floor, where it comes to a halt, and can rest, at last, leaking its sky at the frame, exuding it, on the carpet, which turns blue, as if, but you are on the other side already, don't be scared, it has ceased to exist. I roll up the end of the road where I gulp down the head I was absently chewing; nothing arrives in the dead and buried liberal afternoon to relieve me. I wander the back roads of thinking it out like the cleaner who soiled her spreadsheet; look to the coming of the double-digit growth rate at dawn in the east. We got through worse, the war was the point, it got us together, there was no time off; you can jump the stockade in a second for less than I get for my life in a week. The losers who scavenge for better are throwing their pampered remains out the pram; I stand by the woman beneath me, doing what your country can do for you. It's ok, you will be ok. It's just that, some time ago, many years, you were constrained to use being dead, saying it, I am dead, for a way of needling back into, still needing, the thing that, under the stairs, in the blessing of a lettered recess, a little compartment of a fishing tackle box fitted with a snug of cotton wool, nestling in the last lap of breathable pure cellulose, that ideal pleasures vainly antedate, what are you doing here, what are you doing later, look at it this way, how you are meant to, not at a distance, and say how much you wanted it, and what a simple thing it would have been to have had it, in reality, that body, and to have rubbed it all over yourself, to grow into, in the bathroom with the door locked, cuffed to the towel rail, with some other child banging on the door and telling you to get out.

2

I'm listening. Just stop. When you're ready. I'm listening and I can't help you, your fruit's *verscherʒt*. What shapes? The class struggle has outlived programmatism, and different shapes now inhabit its horizon. What shapes? Truncage, truncature. Look I've stopped listening. Not splitting Communication as till Communication starts out as distress fit audit Zoonotic *notes inégales*. The lineaments, the gratinated gyrus. To your corner, to your corner with the milk thistle gartered in peelable chicken wire, to bug it, the better to bug it with wonder whist, surveil the doloriferous, the punctured, the category, the gloop, the screwed. Who stuff the trachenchyma like cannoli. Historicizing Zolax, leave the point to me, Dionysiokolax, dark tartuffery. Not at work today? No, and you, not visible today? To your platform, to your platform with the anime buzzard's beloved's pinchfisted conatus, too thinkably contused, just not right now. Who drift off to deplore its bolted under Afters flit across the pane, misted up to feel like the crack slipped off again back to somewhere real. Once *I can't* there go feel blue-chip meat. As, just stop. Go ahead. As the last quadrature of sanctuary from the (now it is only a dream) beaked hook's snapped point's discreetly self crossed out, to devastate your duct up with the Benjylitic bargepole of self-evidently ludibrious makeshift gympie gympie, look at me, do I look scared, do you want to fuck, do you hear that. *Pulcher et fortissimus*, leave the world alone, humanity's hissing us, reality's gone. To your crossing, to your crossing with the fake cowpat's fat flock of spectrous vegetating shadow logs and stock stifled parasympathetic canned laughter. Inside the real bedroom under the real bed there is no fucking headroom for my fucking head. Glebously flinch and the Put tar D up snap hope apart put a dent or foot in your head cross (3) look at me, space is shut, try and jump out. Balked by turns the feebly-whistling grass will not be corrected, you bantam salivary duct, all winch and squeaky cleat, meanwhile, ablative, Babaginda, I said look at me, if not you then who, or else, quick, pull, off the top of your head. To your wall peg, to your wall peg, to suck in your punchbag and flop out your tibiotarsus, now wait a million years for the desoldering pump definitely on its way to caress your subprime cut of Pacinian corpuscle with its mis-sold gross anti-static. In benthal receivership trot to the fringe, sanity scratchings for brains. Benjy you blubbery prick stick to squealing, the future is after you, look out the floor's on its way. Your phospholipids are falling out you arpeggiated bray of old agony, to your intersection and cup there your droop of acousticofacial dip, without stickage, without demurs, swivel this way and wait up for my feel (9) to aerify harpoon of random hydrophylloideae. Art world politics take note, history will come, coughed up from your father's throat on Elysium. To your lunchbox, to your lunchbox with the conspicuously undefrosted rectangles of butter jaggedly dug in to the basic white bread, fissile to lick up the thatched sluice of boiling Bonjela, dear origin and ender, dear pig-eyed dumb nociceptualist with the resurfaced trapdoor in your mouth like a recyclable cocaine ball-gag repurposed into a bratty brain prod where love is no object. Look up at the foaming sky pouring life away, how to go on, what to try, difficult to say. Plaited into this un-guilt stem vision for modification by keyhole high spear-grass brass sky needled to slay in fear extinction symbolic inspired blowout the wrong dendritic spine. Aquí te amo, your hojas de alambre, Benya, your petrific enchantment. Blanked like an ankle sock. Eared. When later, decades on. Jack is having some kind of seizure and a fuckload of glue is being suctioned out of his nose, that white glue from the stock cupboard that you stole at primary school, everyone did, that you were given when you were there, to do pictures, *Bildung*, his septum is being corroded; it looks like pleasure, from over here, woozily disauthenticating its gluey ass backwards into reality; he jerks his head back, into light, dripping that fat white stupid glue everywhere, likened to a snowblind tray of fudge, stuck for a code, saying, what do you say, so you say Forgive me, then, Forget me, but you don't really mean it. The worker had to be laid off from the job of revolutionary subject of history, after the allegations of Postone and the last nail of reputational damage in the recalled fluffy Trotsky, to take up being a pain in the university. But the truth is poor people are better than rich people. A simple *modus ponens* inference to Uber's slaves, in the brain congealing like a soup of flooded graves. The time is near when I go back to stacking up your shelves, in envy of the egos busy shacking up with selves. There simply is more space the more you reach beyond the stars, for distance to appropriate, put away your scars. Imprisoned like shellfish said Plato, speaking for the west, born of a mother before him whose Ursatz knows best. In retrospect love is a banner you too soon unfurled, to end up looking for dead ends in every corner of the world, gaslighting the police like a deleted screengrab of the flare-up of a Mattel LED button light. You had one on the Argos calculator you had at school. Don't stop, I'm still listening. What makes this memory's moth's scream's tone's point useful is the great flame of *misery poverty privity laxity* it sports in, that time alone will burn off like a calorie in hell. Yes. Go on. For communization read pick your direction of travel. Don't wait for a heaven where parking will never run out. Hope is pegged to going on regardless, a loss leader, deathlessness's dipshit PA, and everyone left is the plot twist that doesn't add up. Go. You don't get to pick your assassin, despicable asshole. It gnaws through the crack and lays eggs in your AYPI. That noon we flipped out to the horizon coating the treeline, receding in tandem with it under the projected flap of coal. One head shoots out of the other, that one too long ago shot to fuck before it stood in for itself. Before you gave it a chance, in other words.

Only when its truth's spit out is her pain this specific,
Now the night is sober on a plank too low to bleed
O overlong desired only point you first remember

When it hurts, that the least wind dissembles like water
Backed up for the void to barrel out. Every word of this
Scolds the will to hear its infantile phonation ring,

Real, out of its mind, therefore of its misery, here below,
On an empty stomach in the distribution centre
Desperate to stick out when the future's redirected.

Track the language as it thickly laminates the eyelid
To a body never meant to see your light go out.
I will love you until I die and try to be the thing you need.

The mind first has to pick the right reality to limp after,
Ringing in the true the moment evil is corrected,
Mashing up Wednesday so that even the abyss can swallow it,

Which only goes to show that sorrow isn't what it means.
I never could believe that love didn't have to kill me
Stuck to the fence behind the scrap of trees, in progress

Past the children shouting at the knife, over the dogshit
To the limit of the little rectangle of grass
Provided for the local recreation of the poor

Where I had to run away with you when you scooped me
At night to watch you dying, stuffing pills into
The stomach I would take to be pumped so I could live

Right up to the far kerb of the prohairetic blank
Where politics takes over and the secret earth is turning,
So bright it cannot but enlarge the organ that contemplates it.

Only think of power and the theft of the potential
Even from the moon, flipside of every loose incisor
Twisted in a dream prescreening vision for fantasy,

Babeuf went to the guillotine and nobody is right
The structure has a centre surreptitiously assumed
To guarantee the meaning of the whole structure as such.

Back of unstuck Euclid, viols panting like a blowfly,
Nobody is coming to take you home, even later,
Only her departure is held up, but fuck the galaxy.

Know that when you learn to speak reality is coded,
And that being real means feeling like it has to end.
It has to end and you will be alone: the final light.

Down in the iron law of wages, topless pit of rust,
I reach down for the radiant shapes of sleep, as for fire
To gutter on the mirror I have never overlooked,

But have always strained to love, or even care
Painte on flowdes, till the shore, wait, crye to th'ayre
I want to take you to another body with me tonight

Socializing the liabilities of the core, floating ideas
Past the last hour of this sun's resuscitating glory
Out on the steep schizoid rim, plaster cascading in Araby,

Blanked by desire bewildered and errorless, but bent into,
Where life at length inhales all love continually
Despite living in poverty and not always eating,

Being put behind you, being sadly beaten up,
Scared to say what is happening, terrified in case it is
Back and you go fucking mad and kill someone.

We are come to the far-bounding plain of earth. Void of
state. Personologized. Fact-finding. *Mira de lente.* Not
once a credible counterparty in the CDS. Snoring in the
lake of mud. Making eye contact by staring. Before
they are sent back, to the disgrace of death, to face the
owner of the reference assets (often the originator),
breviloquent, ithyphallic, think of the flower, cut to a
symbol, printed in a (4) four angle a river flowing over
infant spicules bursting ever slower to a shore where
you, simultaneously cut down, to make a bunch, left
agreeing to pay the swap counterparty premiums based
on the perceived probability of credit events occurring
in the reference assets, with your pants down, inflated
by susurrus, one long since already put away but now
recalled because combustible toy at a time, look away,
don't be shy, since, according to the replacement for Ian
Duncan Smith, behind every statistic there is a human
being, as a support mechanism, ready to pounce, shod
in inflammable memory foam, happy to get out, for a bit,
when, though it is safe to say never, since the size of the
notional (7), it aerifys market in mid-2007 was roughly
twice the size of the U.S. stock market (valued at about $22

trillion) and thus far exceeded the $7.1 trillion mortgage market and hole sealed $4.4 trillion U.S. treasuries market, in what flows of syrupy Syrians sweetly mock, in vain, before being sent back, to pick that flower, lick that symbol, pucker to a torus nailed to a stent, printed in a river of outstretched seconds burst through to cut, to light, to look up at, a productively lost but prokaryotic parody of a hedge with a massive gaping mouth, a saw for teeth and a tongue of gelatinous genitals peaking in berries and cross-flitting swallows, obligated to glisten from the muck, on hunger strike in paradise, disgusted of nowhere, sat on as a joke, it is safe to say, as a result, that the swap counterparty should gain exposure to the risks attached to the reference assets without title or any other rights in them passing to it, whatever, fine, but who, for all that second alike, even at that fork as nothing by comparison with the vital principle of permanency, down on its luck, I might not tell everybody, but I will tell you that caused such mad potent surges to erupt in me, and that made such exuberant, intense interiorities suddenly flare, that I would have palpitations, terrified that my heart would explode, and how it set up this question over and over again at a thousand different angles, pushing past and rejecting anything that sounded like an answer, to pit against the state of sound, that you try to forget, holding out for an answer that cannot be got, because it's heard when it's not given. Indurated, the ultimate macroaggression Benjy *animo nudo* shrieks for, his skull in a flap, clean your brie, now poetry, quarter-inching by spiteful entrechats over to the pickled guard rail with a twist of nettle-tip sticking out my fingernail, with which to spear his frantic eye, Benjy of the apes, a human bauble of delirium, merely wild with fear, prematurely flinching like a crab in creosote, or like snow, fresh pressed by elk's hoof, where you go, the names agree, in our ears, bendy

Benjy's surplus splurpy, cut with other sound, born to hurt, to pinch, to flick away. Here is the interpretation of your dream. The *orange pump* is the *tube in an inflatable life vest* that you squeeze and blow into to stop drowning. Blowing into it when asked is the symbol for *being invited to pause* under your breath midway through the line of the Old Arcadia if you want the job enough. It's obvious you do want the job because deep down you don't know whether you would sooner breathe or die. The utility model discloses (4) four angle junctions of an inflatable life, (4), of inflatable unit have cross vest of defending oneself, life vest distribution a plurality of inflatable unit (3), cross (3) have four blow vent (13), stretch into adjacent four respectively inflatable unit (4), be close to collar (1) has been located the mouth and has been blown up the formula and aerify hole (5), the mouth blows the formula and aerifys hole (5) and have the mouth and blow the formula and aerify hole sealed cap (6), life vest left side lower part branch is equipped with inflates gas casket (7), it aerifys hole (8) and has and aerify the gas casket and aerify hole switch (9) to aerify the gas casket, life vest right side lower part is set up separately and is responded gas casket (10), reaction gas casket (10) has reaction gas casket and aerifys hole (11), therein lies the utility model as it discloses simple structure, scientific and reasonable, stop it, put your mind away, the mode of aerifying of three kinds of difference, convenient and fast, and in the sea, ostensibly sticky Benjy, ostensibly convertible, whose unbounded sway, that day adagiodigitated on the living room sofa, yet at bay, strung up like a sackcloth of goat-hair, nailed like a tongue's tip to the sky.

3

Today is your birthday, Benjy, and your mother and I have built you a wall of presents, up to the ceiling, that transversally bisects the front room from corner to corner, and when you go running in all your friends will be waiting for you on the other side, to clap as you headbutt your way out, and the presents collapse, and you can open them after. It's a surprise, don't spoil it. Once in you will note the effulgence befitting the modesty of the only window, by which it is irradiantly gilted, how you like, and before which, the little throng, arrangement, or composition, of your friends, looms, silhouetted out of their pre-negligible minds, teeny, identified, wincy, parakinesic, massed at the cargo scanner over by the watch list, where you dug your thumbs into the wall. That is the window which shulde elles springe unto the worldes knoulechinge, except that you are shortly to be bundled out of it to be pictured smiling by the bush of pampas or ribbon grass, on one unfaded random blade of which, secret still, for its and your safekeeping, to this day abides the lick of blood left over from when you went and sliced into the taut skin you hate between the thumb and proximal crease of the index finger of the little sibling who, nicked, cried a bit, when you did it first and they copied you, no society can be stable unless there is a basic core of value judgments that are unthinkingly accepted by the great bulk of its members, *O miei cari sospiri*. And if you barge in all at once, eyelids flapping, brain akimbo, ass for heels, you'll make it clean through the wall and the little crock of friends too like a blubbery box cutter and fly out the window, an acrobatic exaggeration of your actually predetermined exit velocity, into the deep heart of the bush, where darkness waits like a knitting pattern for light rescaled at length to fit the sky you shed again, to disappear, and reappear at the moment of truth, either side of the moment of *chush'sobach'ya*, where you will find, blindfold, by groping the echoes, that secret blade, and you will extirpate its randomness by wiping the edge down and piecing the fossilized incision back together, you evil pig. Confirmation of this will be carried in triumph back to Whitelands in the un-form of an unobscurable myoclonus. Hoisted by the Barclays. Then it is, yssued of the same wyth herte deuoute bysprange ryghte humbly and by grete loue and ardour of dylection the hostel – *pace* to be, or become, unequal to, or bypass, by negative incapability, either way, as even the most superficial glance at the history of human thought will persuade you, benefited like the stalk, that twineth ecliptically, same old Benjy, same old obviously abjointed disanalogy to even the infinitieth perforation of a hereafter, fucked, in other words, back to yours, more spatter than breath, down behind the train tracks, digging up the pit, laying the coverlet of twigs, buds and leafs over, and leading you by the arm, as if you were blind, and I were kind, to the promised spot of fortune, and watching, totally delighted, as it happens, as you tread on the twigs and fall in, and not even really laughing, but just knowing, for once, the gratification, for that long inestimable instant, of the wish, sordid admittedly, but fulfilled, for enough power to make you do anything, go anywhere, plummet in whatever pit I say, at the bottom of which, as if in a more fundamental window, you should have seen your face, that dumb pout, glistening, Planktos to a Vatican, and seized hold of it and never let go (I dug a hole, knee-deep, covered it in twigs and leafs, led you to it, pretending we were going to see something exciting, you trod on it and fell in). Now, thought, Benjy, is a child begotten by the brain in communion with some object, whose mental effigy, interjaculated by the senses, has a father and a mother, one in the object, and one in the head, where unfortunately you are not allowed in. But you are allowed out. Or you are not allowed out, technically, anyhow not in the too obvious sense, that you mean, but you are given to obtrude there, by being superimposed over a thing that is. And never peeled off. This ought to be relatively painless, provided you feel it. Think a slow, quacking sensation, like a kind of double-dip *verlängerter Selbstmord*, or calamitously dusting an asbestos shoehorn with a colander of icing sugar, every one of whose holes has been plugged with the makeshift of an anaesthetized sleeping wasp, or just soldered shut, after everyone has already gone home. It starts in your layers, creeping up on you, takes hold, and spreads out from there, way, way out, into the other layers. Nobody would blame you. These days the outer layers all come already fixed on, all you do is tip yourself inside. Only you must be careful not to be too heavy, or the wrong way up, or you will smash the layers, fly everywhere, and inscrutably pulverize them back to reality, and then there will be no layers left, not a single one. All those long, forgivable layers, layers of painlessness, layers of specificality, layers of archanalgesia, layers conducive to retirement and the entire exemption from pain, layers of I didn't mean it, of its staying not meant, of *de facto* downright not meantness, or barely, never dredged. But today we are on thought. Thought on the other hand must be in effect distinctified out of the head, like a disinfected bullet casing, from the faculty of thought, with the crest, that, but for its ubiquity, would be forever narrowly missed. Except that, ever more begotten, or else just pigheadedly disinclined to be butchered, when indisposed, once heretofore infinituple, or go out with a trill, or huff, alternating amœbaean microtones, pumped, gooey, defaced by gross, motion-sick salivification, doggy-paddling to sububiquity, shitting your leftovers, it should – meaning thought – on the principle, *neque unquam duo ova, aut duo folia vel gramine, &c.*, that I'm afraid you already consented to, twice, once by fleeing over the hummock, as if mime-screaming, from the killer progenitrix bounding after you with the cartoonishly outsized, antiquitated syringe, jonesing to flush your life out with a fat booster of staring embryos, and once by alternatively being skewered over and over again on the apical bud or sharpened canine of an anonymous stalk, breaks out in what we call pseudopods, figuratively, *fórcole* of the folliculous, to prune, nip, gnaw, chew, spit out, then pick up off the floor, between the tips of your finger and thumb, carefully remove the hairs and bits of dust, and stick back in again, as though nothing had happened, through a hole in the ear, and get over it. Its fruit, inness, then swells, as a sac, or is bloated, for lasciviency, adultomorphic, and fire, don't waste it, you have time, don't be another sot of bismare word, permanently being sent to your room, a mile upstairs, to be cross-bred, to swinge and scuttle, over by the means, along with the task, clipping the object, and the other, as all rise like a wheedled spire of yeast, preppy, paretic, half-joking, naturalesque, only not as hitherto, it's better for you like that, and it's better that you stay, in common with other phenomena, wallowing in time and space, empty, busy, painless, pissy, ignorant, alive, respectfully spooning the void, and, as you begin to feel that familiar burning, way down there, that you admit to yourself, scarily, the truth of it, which is that you can't help it, you're human, the void turns you on, you have always wanted to fuck the void, you have always wanted to make the void come the hardest, you have always wanted the void to tell everyone that you are the best, you have always wanted the void to lean in very close and whisper in your ear, loud enough for everyone to hear, Benjy, you are the best I ever had, and you deserve to be allowed, without hindrance, fact, alternative fact, defection from the ideal, empty or full compliance, dangled off a precipice of infinited sound, left for dead, in a head, mutely deafening, where nothing could be less, or fit to grind, once scutched, a cataract of ossicles, torn a new point, go, handed your desire, and I don't want to hear about who did what, it doesn't matter who did what, or to whom, or when, or with what, who, or in what corner, put it down, put the corner down right now, wherever you like, not there, and which brain function, equally, is no purer than the scent of a flower, of the fields, or of a desk, or of a light, or of the way, in or out, you pick, until it's sore, as who should say, for the active cannot subsist without the passive, but – chin up Benjy, eat your cake – *somebody* has to be the object, the passive, the chair leg, the replacement chair leg, and the whole ungamifiable substrate of pollinators, *ainsi des plantes faibles s'entrelacent ensemble pour résister aux ouragans*, swallow, the naturel hete of blood humayn comforte my, cut it out, somethingness, vegytalle wyth sencyble moeuynges, for must not something, and I'm not naming names, be even these things? that to let by, stop it, to not corrugate, or emitting – frivoling away – a single cry, while sticking your fox cub – braving a hundred lashes of the whip – ripped out the pantry, up under your pyjamas, to be not shamed by being not found out, and able thereafter to justify eating it alive, after everything we do for you, spontaneously the solution. Tip-toe upon the dreary mound, sled-struck, spattered with creosote, past the bolus, over the sex, where, God-fearing, seaworthy, probabilistic, clammy with woe, I first had thought to put myself in you, but, pettifogulizingly post-integrated with its own minute tortuosities of construction, but game, thenceforth senseless, fork me on GitHub, Dean of Allodynia, born to cloud over, to prod at, to rub out like eyes, one more push, for the urethane lateral to go as yet not too torn out discrepant, as of only six lyke a corps wythoute entendemente or else, fed up, let down, felt up, numb in bed, you've barely touched your panic button, please not with your mouth open. Even from the top of the mountain, rutted and covered in ice, the purple drains away, the perishable light of a sun is terminated. Long has night obscured the valley stretched out for the wanderer, he, by the turbulent stream, forever attempting the next hut up, bound for the close of his day, for carefree retirement living. The mystery sleep is obligingly stretched out just as far ahead, keeping it excellent company. I beckon it down quick, here, crown of oblivion, rest on my head. But what is that light extravasated out of that rock, darting into me, that spray from the stream that shines with this unearthliest iridescence? Has the sunlight penetrated the most downreaching cracks, because this lustre is not normal, irradiating conversely. I'm surprised at you, Benjy. You know you're not supposed to be in here, skimmed off like a froth of cashew milk, gnawing on the bars, futilously literal, petitioning the air to let you teethe. Listen to this. The heating up of sounding bodies, just as of beaten or rubbed ones, is the appearance of heat, originating conceptually together with sound. Thought. A haddock umbilicus, poached in tears, doggy-paddling in your joint fluid, terrified of what I will do next, to Egypt, where, soft-shelled, braindead, from across the policing family, your missing ends between its teeth, pulled to make a bow. In flights of reactionary fire veined with obsidian and elastic, madly

tarsal, you lay on my lap and I bend down to lick your
eternity shines in the map of my sky, where there is
mutual respect among all employees, regardless of official
statuses, and when what employees will ultimately not
have to be afraid to say suggests ideas to improve the
work processes, benefiting everyone in the return. Your
driver is called Benjy, they've just picked up your order.
But issuing from the self-anchored control room with the
wilted truss dug out of the occulted core of the panic
room with the predictably defaced GRP ballistic screen
dotted with the prudently abandoned beginnings of
eyeholes that stick out like leaf galls in 1992, the voice
of a steel bust of Ihor Kolomoisky, last assiduously
hallucinated assiduously dripping in Kremenchuk
existiculae, delivers the colourful laugh track of
adjectives again: *beheaded, nowise, hasbeen, deboning, noo
lenger.* Spraying lumps of bollocked molar, making the
real eye mist up like a yummy mudflap; for once, hold off
going there, where it is so easy to hide and be pretentiously
reckless, while actually breaking, and turning all your
oratory sour, and losing sight of where, but hearing, like
a rumour, the love song of absorbefacient dissolution,
and singing it to yourself, and really hearing it in all the
music that you love, where your life really is, in the sense
that, though it can't be lived, it can be heard and listened
to, and you can sit and listen to it in silence, shut the
window, turn the light out, cover your eyes to heal the
darkness, and know, for so long as you can still contact
the reality that you are hearing, that it therefore loves
you, and that you and it are the same: you are real too.
How else go down to the bad titratable rim or bashed flap
of cytoplasm and its limit to a life wiped out, scatebrous,
chewy, old, illicit, lorded over by the railing, waved
through? I grasp my reeking 8H, flatten your card on the
pluckable wrist, tease out the badge with the safety pin

and cartoon balloon number 6, fling it on the table, and
write, Fuck you, Benjy. You hurt people too often and
repeat / the history you kill yourself to stop / to make
yourself the predator you need; / but don't discount the
dream of getting out: / there is no other exit but your
head. Then I rephrase that. The cloud becomes intimate,
glowing. Amazed, I scrutinize the wonder. Doesn't the
ray of rouge light cast a properly berserk shadow? Lid,
id scriptor, soft abode, pleasure's node, licking that
Unhinged door, Bearing in mind This night that I stare
at Licking that Face to be kind, it's torn too, to work,
born To be torn Licking that Points to you. Then you
will run back in crying the same thing she is, pretending
you both did it at the same time — see, the departed
returns, through forests and hideousship's overhangs —
that your cut is the same as hers, and equally deserving of
what pity and love there is to go round, scant as it is,
rather than what you know it is in reality.

Starting from low the light ascends in a single slow movement,
So that sight is lifted the distance up to the tilting board.
On top of the board is a pair of bodies, one on top of the other.

One of the bodies is still alive, the other is beneath her.
She cranes the little distance down to brush it with her mouth
And bring it back to meaning, bites to resurrect the cord.

Implicit in everything, you are the only reason it expresses,
Watching in the role of sight, lifted without acknowledgment.
The top body renounces its enigma to make sense of you.

It's an animal that hovers above a corpse of its own making,
The child beneath her, but too hurt by its non-disclosure,
Recoils to think of Bronstein in his grave with no encouragement.

It looks for a single way past but it can't find it, as if paralysed,
Gently clawing at the patch of motionless second body,
Able to say what it wants by first moving its top head down.

It only wants to speak and for the thing that died beneath it
To be made to hear and for the meaning to be analysed
To make everything mean everything it could, to that body.

The role of sight expands to fill the pocket of its brief
Exposure to the vision this exchange of fear symbolizes,
Balling up their feathers to a moon behind the eye,

Where nothing they can say can ever change beyond this cry.
From now on they do this, one on top, one under it,
Matching exhaustion to the missing future it cannibalizes.

Starting from here the lights go up in attenuated movement,
So that sight can spot the difference on the tilting board.
On top of the board is a pair of bodies, one on top of the other.

Both of the bodies are still alive. Her child is beneath her.
She bends the little distance down to feel it on her mouth
And bear with it for meaning, breathes vibration to the cord.

Explicit in everything, you are the only reason it releases,
Living in the sun of sight, gifted without acknowledgment.
The top body pronounces its enigma to make sense of you.

A tree that stands above a ground now of its own making,
The child beside her, but too close for its long disclosure,
Rebounds to antic Bronstein in his grave without his nourishment.

It looks for a shorter way past and it can't find it, as if paralysed,
Gently doting on the motion of the fiftieth body,
Ready to be everything it wants lost by moving its head down.

It only wants to say that once the thing that died within it
To be made to hear and for the meaning to be analysed
To make everything clear, is everything enough, to that body.

The end of sight extends to film the socket of its brief
Exposure to the vision this exchange of hope finalizes,
Balling up their feathers to a moon behind the eye,

Where nothing they can say can ever change beyond this cry.
From now on they do this, one on top, one under it,
Matching exhaustion to the static future it containerizes.

No way is more in than out, this time, that, in the end,
slowed down to make it sad, migrated to a stratum at
the low point of the tinsel actin network that, intrinsic,
condoned, done up by obsessive fiddling, screwed
to memory at a loss, that, one too many twisted times
attempted in the dark, loosed beyond retightening the
rivet of that blood rotating on the crater bed or catapulted
in a vacant arc, that is a seal. For what, now that you
think of it, is what, outward utensils, since you do not,
you are free to go. The point is to untwist the end off
first, *sempre con fuoco*. Then rot in the contingent. Sailing
the seven seas. Stealing aboard containers. Fucked,
pulling its hair out. Watching truth forced up, forced
out. Be careful, it might be forced out too far. Or be
put out. To where it will not be able to be clawed back.
That picture it destroy what can be loved. It might be
forced out so far that anyone could get in, irrespective of
qualities, mouthfeel, future earnings, creed, or viscosity,
by swooping down the core. Delusion is always floating.
Inwardizing grit. In conformity with the necessity of
its development. Propping up the roof, letting down
the floor, sick of its droning, bored to shreds, even now

reducible in some dead part to nothing but in order to be pure at all or change, or else things would never change, so that, and so long as, hard-pressed, untumultuous, with an unobstructed internal view, you see what you would be if there were nothing but the truth for life and counting, keeping meaning close, paranoid it will fade, as everything once held did inside the distance racked up to the vapid obstacle of being here where sound is left, subcutaneous, bereft of limits, starved on dreams, come again, but backlit, to be taught its lesson, the one, going back to what you first, listening for what is true, sped up to make it funny, the sunk costs of sanity, as a storm-tossed vessel in a sea of anything, adamantly drifting out of view, on the drive out, to feel confiscated, born to be phanerogamic, panic-induced, to allow one beautiful thought, where, to become shallower, dying I make last until, restores tranquility, tastes like shit, assuming demand, that, on credit, razes out the troubled brain, ingrown, ominously normal, lived to bits, one, to feel gone, one way, to be ended, or grow new. When, shaking the end of the night back into the flesh, scattering grated glass over the blocked sink bolted on the common, raising its eyes to mine, I seemed to feel true, make a sign now meant for you, as what it empties into is the overturned car again barely tender, the wish without end that to stop it dying I make last until it is a specific life scooped out, whose one time, integral to its yield, we are here to go on with, where, aged naked, studying what we owe, in order not to let go, and how to make do with it: final prices were significantly lower. USD 148 million for the 5 year and 7.5 year bucket respectively; downturns become shallower. The short list of deliverable obligations led to a scarcity of available securities in the 2.5 year bucket, nature is dead anyway. This shortage exacerbated by high demand in Thomson bonds, due to the inclusion *now a dim speck, now vanishing in light* of Thomson in off-the-run iTraxx Europe indexes small sell open interest of the 2.5 year bucket USD 80.967 million exhausted by a single order exactly equal to the open interest posted by J.P. Morgan at a very high bid of 96.25%. And I feel now the future in the instant. And overall the battle ebbs and flows. Vomit emptiness. Ending with a high recovery allows low payments for cash settlements, which would be rational for J.P. Morgan. In consequence on floated bonds abroad, a larger number of bid orders was needed, exhaust these open interests to sell, to shrink the final price, inscribing a payer option to reduce the cost of holding a short position in the underlying index, misusing this strategy, one cost of index short, but in turn, to give up some of the upside from spread widening, to illustrate this strategy with one simple example.

4

I cannot pretend to be
Done yet with this random life
That you never wanted for

Any thing that can suffer
Either. I can't write except
In a stupor of the time

We got wasted every day
With no other idea why
But that the intensity

Makes up for the pain at last
And that love is easier
In a blindness really lived.

I will be forgiven this
In a sensitive abyss
Too long not missed, in the way

Your sound will turn out to be
Hid in every other sound,
Not even mine. Listen out:

Originally magic
Floating numbers marginal
Liberally infloresced

Now garland the moon, except
Not in this life, only too
Soon foregone and overdue,

Sighted in a wilderness
Of staples in a block of
Lard, specific, void, too near

For you every motion is
Too far, to the horizon
That rebuts the sky with us.

But here we are. You are not
Alone any more now that
No one's left. And nothing changed:

We're still here, we're still apart,
We're still going to die, but
You did everything you could.

*

What we wanted was this world
To stop and whatever is
Next to start love all over

Again but no poverty
This time or victimized past
For one life on end but not

Parodied by dying too
Soon. That it's too much to ask
Since this world is all we get

It was hard to know, given
That it is not true. The way
You talk you would think you live

Every life there is except
Yours. And I know you really
Do or get to better than

I do, who will never get
Why it should be lived at all
Once the start is fucked up but

Once is enough. The real sky
Stands still, the darkness is fresh
Like milk in a mere syringe,

Starvation's infinity
Flutters, a pennon of blood
Still high the instant we die

Flying the world like a kite.
Know you said in a way no
One else did yet what pain is.

*

This is how it seems to me
Anyhow, and since I'm still
Here I get to pick the words

For the nonexistent sound
To proof your void. Back to back,
We are fucking in a dream

Every spasm consequent
Further back, it's like getting
High but not totally trashed

Oblivion on earth. We
Go in fury till the end
Left blank for us to fill in.

This is my first dream of you,
I will take good care of it.
Cut up into ocean floors

Of time, that trickles down, leased
Back, redistributed, sane,
Coiled, for ease, less facile, quick

To peel, free to freeze until
The fatal day it boils. Our
Arms are flippantly ripped off,

Mine by yours and yours by mine
All for good, we never end,
In the dream we will forget

To have, or know is real, here,
Down the psyche, shivering,
Curled up to be analyzed

Ultimately to be loved.
Free again another day
In another way bereft,

And don't come back. As I lose
Sight of you the air will thin
Dug in infancy to feel,

On a brittle eminence,
Adolescenter logic
Start its sore ascent, lyric

Take remediable flight
To a hundred places where
I scorn to go. Plongid up,

Words to fill out, in a row
That, sticking to the window
Like light, that first instructed

Me, like water in a jar,
What it means to really stop
Imperviously emptied

Just by falling on my eye
Staring past it at outside.
This is it again, the same.

At that intact window I
Opened on to nothing left.
Now I can jump out of it.

Today was such a beautiful day with you. I was anxious,
on the drive out, that you would be sick again, and I had
to dart my eyes about, as the road, already narrow, but
more constricted because of the cars parked all along the
kerb, curved round and swung, looking for places where
I could pull over and stop in case you did, and I couldn't
see any. But I felt the way I think I would feel if I knew
you would be ok, and as if, really, I didn't have to look,
because we wouldn't have to stop, but I looked anyhow, to
be kind, and to be seen to be kind. In the end we got there

quick and you were fine. I turned in, over the dugout in the middle of the entry, between the posts, and parked over by the side, far back enough for whoever it was in front to get out easily, without the distress of feeling like they were being tested on their skills in front of whoever might be sitting next to them, or having to worry that they might clip me, when there was no need, because, for the moment at least, there was room enough for everybody. I got out and opened your door to let you out and as soon as I put you down you wanted to run away as fast as you could, to anywhere there was, to everywhere, and I was to pretend that I was running fast too, to keep up with you, and that it was a race and that one of us would win. You would win, because, but now in words, I love nothing in my life so much as for you to be delighted, and because I have not found in myself the least desire ever to be ahead of you, or to have anything that you do not, or get anywhere you couldn't get to, how would I even look, but my whole body, and even, as it really did feel, my whole being, which could be felt throughout me, like a dizziness, panic, or great tide, swelled with a mad joy I could barely hold, to see you even one millimetre in front of me, or a split second ahead, running, waving and shouting. The point of the race was that you would win. You hadn't seen grass for a long time, for days, and when you ran off into the grass that was thick, dark, and swept up off the earth by the breeze, you began screaming the word grass, really ecstatically, over and over again, *grass*, *grass*, and running in wild circles through it and catching at it with your fingers. Exhilaration too new to be happiness yet, but bound there, flooded your face, your fingers, your hair, your eyes. You are the most beautiful person I have seen, the most beautiful thing I have touched. I watch you and I think to myself you are so beautiful, that simply being here to share this definitely finite piece of existence with you, even with everything that is going on, is about as much beauty as I can take, or more beauty than I can take, more than I could ever get through, and though it is enough simply to be here with you, and in your presence, without knowing or caring about anything, but only knowing that what you are to me is more than I could ever be to myself, I can't resist the other thought, too, that I have learned something, and that now I know, despite even now having no idea how to stop wanting to destroy myself, that being with you, and being able to feel in every part of myself that you are there, and being here for no imaginable greater purpose than to love you, the way I truly do, is also how to justify my life.

Out of nowhere yet as if almost cardboard, but for the outline, half as if in marker pen, only too candescent, I am on a night out with Starsy. Everything I am about to say is not meant to be in words, that's the whole point. The picture plane is at a subtle tilt, backwards a fraction into space, a very acute angle. A few steps ahead of us, as we go jerkily along, he behind me and to the right, I with my head rotated to left, twisted as if it had come off a hundred times but had always been stuck back on and had gone all the way round this time to heed what he is saying, to everything and nothing of which I pay minute attention, although struggling to pretend I am not bemused, because, it is Starsy, who could kill me. Starsy only comes into the world to kill me, otherwise he doesn't come into it, and whatever else he may think he gets up to is nothing but a wet dream from which he never wakes up. Floribund, invertebrate full-stop. Obviously I could, with the sang-froid of an aborted nimrod, shake him, throw water over his face, or even go at him with the frozen waffle and egg, to irritate the lungs and trigger an inhalation reflex to elevate the blood oxygen levels, without a creeping thing like that being any the wiser, but then it is certain he would kill me. He used to hog the bathroom and take ages weirdly trying to look good, our Lord, fishing for supplicants, but now you are the bathroom and the hair gel and the bathroom mirror, and light falls in through the extractor. The night out commences in trepidation, signified by augury; all over its polluted darkness flicker the shadows of the reservoir of fire, tiresomely surreal. But Starsy turns out to be weirdly excellent company, practically saluberrime. In among the scrap spreads, cherrypick the specks, approached mnd presented tomet I had written, but somsthough frightningly reorganized into gible; too thought, how could she have known that, even I didn't know, and I'd done it, when I was out of my fucking mind; henceﬂes banished, by the police; but she did, next something madme go out into the road, to a blind corner, tha hugged the cliff, round which the frozen waﬄe and egg, or bodies pop out like felt cut-outs, or picture cards, snapping for an instant and straight back in again, behind the cliff; she made me go rounthacorner, where a heinous, bloated man whose hard ﬂesh all but split out, familiarly, of his pink or purple skin who had eyes red or orange dead and seafood lunged at me, and I swung at him a sheet of cardboard, medium size, and it lolloped through the wind at his head, ineﬀectually scooped away from impact; and at the instant when it was supposed to hit his head an articulated lorry went ﬂying into him instead and smeared the head into the distance. I wonder what is going on where Starsy is taking us. We sit, facing, across a low desk, a Mexican, or Colombian, or Venezuelan, murderer, from the cartel, who has waited in an empty room, or hangar, the walls of which are grey, or blue, and all of which is either vast or, likewise, conﬁning like a cell. Starsy and I are in trouble, and we both think, I don't want to be here, but we are not going to be wiped out. We are not going to be like things that you break and are made to pay for. The Mexican murderer tells us that we were caught having our night out and now we work for him. But it seems clear the night was set up to lead to this. Starsy and I are in the same boat. We are both conscious that neither of us need be more conscious of its ulterior undulation than the other. That doesn't last long. There is nothing to be said, only the framework of a self-explanation: being able to identify who is sitting opposite, seeing the walls, being able to identify their colour, or its shade, being told that you have been caught, our reaction to it, and the moment. Anyone sitting in that seat is someone you could learn to forget, a hundred times, or, honestly, a thousand times, at least, but whoever it is doesn't matter, what matters is that you did it. There is no door, but you are out the door. The next morning me and Starsy are in bed. We are awake at the same moment. It is the morning but it is still night, or still the afternoon, only very early. There is someone new, there, lying in between us. Each of us reaches his arm toward the other, over this person whose body separates us and has brought us together like this, actually reaching, having to reach, for each other, and letting our arms mingle, or shoulders clasp, and not collide, at a point above the new body, where even he is no longer going to kill me, and where for once I can't, but am happy that he's there. To the person between us we owe the possibility of this touching, at the point of waking, that need not be caressing to be love, or strangling, or clawing, and we know we do. It is not a new start, but the coming together of what has really only been off somewhere else, a bit too permanently, and too long, like a dead mouth. But even a dead mouth can be softly prised open to disclose a perfectly living mouth that has been going on talking all this time. And it's amazing that something finally did it, after so many years

of begging, blindly, for who knows what the fuck, and so
many millions of seconds clinging on like an equilibrist
by the fingernails to the rotten fraction of a ledge of air,
chewing on a plank of molar wrist, and that it was done
to me, using Starsy, who is now also me. All that matters
is that there is somebody in the world who can, or once
did, lie down like that, between even an abyss like Starsy,
who, no less abyssal, apparently now loves me, and me,
and who really does, not sustainably, but right now, so
that it is still there whenever you open your eyes, make
the world the place for love, at last.

*

It is really good to see
You looking so well at last.
Come here so I can hold you

Up to the light that I have
Kept for when you are ready
To use it. I have been gone

Too, but we are both here now
And there is no reason why
We can't stay here if we like

It here and hold on to each
Other. You don't need to tell
Me again what you did or

Couldn't not do or how it
Wasn't you or try again
To hold the rift together

Any more and nor will I
Need it or try to do it
For you on my own as if

I had to be both of us
Or else it would never end
Every night. I will stop it

Too and not go on as if
I could never believe you
Really even had a mind

Left under that sanity
To hear speaking for itself
Of its tragic love for me

That I could ever hear out.
It is our time to let go.
Hold me while I leave you here.

*

It is easier to say
Than words can be got to do.
All you do is stay alive.

It is difficult to say
What this is for. Once a sound
Is found for loss the loss is

Too far off to turn it down
Like the volume of the sky
Split up into echoes by

The head whose cry it catches
As it still collapses. Here
Where there is no point in that

Ancient gist of pain still it
Strung out in the void again
Plastered with musical gore

Off and on kicks in the door
Spiting its detested hinge
Fanned away in old Fukang

To the corner of the room,
Where the microtargeted
Do obeisance extinctly

One step forward at a time,
Pavans, splints, paralysis,
Until it is up for them

Notwithstanding how it flies
To get over it for once
For the poor violent children

That you liked at school who now
Do jobs you hate for them to
Do in fantasy for you

Who don't mean anything to
Them now. As you lift the lid
On another system whose

Moons are suns, whose other skies'
Gravities prevail, for this
Spiraloid discoherence

And try to bear in mind their
Vacuolation by grind,
Make words to look up to flood

The air as far as life boxed
Into the abyss can tell,
Because they are not alone

So it can be tracked. And if
By still going on like this
You are trying to go home

To a mother who will not
Stop committing suicide
That you have to take to A

And E in an ambulance
When you have school the next day
Nothing is going to change

That. It is caught up in why
All the things you always say
Keep the pain they mock in play

Till it is no longer sore
And, emboldened, you reply
I don't want to any more.

*

In the end I don't know what
Else to overwrite you with
But this. In another world

Left to rot in fantasy
Like this one, identical,
Except you were made for it,

Fly regression to the fount
Of pain learnt, start to finish,
Back to front, at peace to be

Where old rain lashes the glass
Like spit in the face of me
Dreaming of a brick. Speak out

Potessi dirti pria
Ch'io mora – if I could
Let you know before I die

How it feels. But I don't know.
They who one another keep
Still alive, n'er parted be,

For poetry will survive
On cracks, deep, true, crisp and flat
Graved into the yielding top

Front brain you got to fuck up
Long ago, full of plastic
Like the sea, poetic, dire,

Drying out, fissile, brassy,
Stupidly irascible
As your head is passed around

Scuffed up in the disbelief
That it would ever come off
Despite the obvious, far

Noises in the lonely trees.
If you look hard you can see
Us there. And please also know

That you did more to repair
Than kill us, as if to spite
A self that never will sing

That did sing. Still alive, hear
Love echo. Even here, like
Laughter, any second now.

ACKNOWLEDGMENTS

'Sinking Feeling' was first published in *Whither Russia*, London:
Barque, 2017. An early draft of scherzo 3 was published online by
the87press in their 'Digital Poetics' series in May 2020. My thanks
to Azad Ashim Sharma. Some of the tercets of scherzo 3 appeared
in the exhibition *Moral Support* by Stephen G. Rhodes and Keston
Sutherland at the gallery 650mAh in Hove, UK, September 16–
November 10, 2018. My thanks to Ella Fleck and Tabitha Steinberg.